PYTHON

Easy Python Programming for Beginners

Your Step-By-Step Guide to Learning
Python Programming

Felix Alvaro

Acknowledgments

Firstly, I want to thank God for giving me the knowledge and inspiration to put this informative book together. I also want to thank my parents, my brothers and my partner Silvia for their support.

Table of Contents

Introduction

Congratulations on downloading this guide! You are one of a few people that take their learning seriously and actually make the first step to learning such an amazing programming language such as Python. By downloading this book, you will not only be able to learn the basics of coding language, but you will also excel and have complete control on this technology.

You have to be aware that you're about to do something you couldn't do before, whether it is out of fear, or perhaps out of doubt in your own abilities. It's true that Coding might sound complex and extremely complicated at first sight. And there is no denying that some people don't even dare to give it a chance. But now, that you have this step-by-step guideline, none of that actually matters anymore. For what you are about to learn, following the steps in this book, is absolutely incredible. Those steps are in fact easy, simple and straight to the point. You do not need to have any specific background whatsoever in order to grasp them. All the answers to your future questions using Python are simply here, well detailed and incredibly accurate.

If you're starting from scratch, every time you will write a code, you're going to be mesmerized. It will keep pushing you constantly to dive even further into it. And believe it or not, only then will you realize that you are able to do more, to manipulate the coding and to transform it as you please. The point is, you will see yourself improving as this training progresses. All you will have to do is to always take the next step and your progress will astonish you. You will be amazed how easy and reachable this art of technology is! What you certainly must know is that when it comes to Python there is no experience required. So if you have never wrote a line of code, this is the perfect place to start. What makes this book completely different from the other guides is that it accompanies you through every step you take from the very first start and guides you gently throughout all the basics.

As we all know, programming is now one of the most powerful tools to solve different kinds of problems. All fields are now inescapably touched by this technology. You have a small business and you're curious to know if this business of yours is thriving according to social media? You can go out there and write your own code to collect tweets, shares and likes. You need to buy a house, a car, or even a yacht and you can't figure out how to handle your money? Python would help you calculate how much you need to save for over 3 or 5 years. You won't need your bank counsellor anymore; you will be your own! It's amazing what one can do once they get a grasp of this technology.

I can promise you that once you have followed the instructions included in this book and carefully practiced every bit of them, coding won't represent a problem for you anymore. It will on the other hand be the embodiment of a new won challenge, and most importantly, one that would make your daily life so much easier and incredibly neater.

Python is a wonderful programming language. It is modern, portable, powerful and above all easy to learn. Don't just sit there and surrender to your fears of possible future failures. Because that is unlikely to be an option in your case. Of course not, now that you have this book at your fingertips. Go ahead and give it a shot, I promise that you won't have the slightest regret. Rather be grateful to this amazing new tool at your reach.

In the first chapter you will learn about the history of Python, what it is mainly used for, its benefits and what makes it better than other languages.

Let's get to it!

Chapter One: What is Python?

In this chapter you will learn about the history of Python, what it is mainly used for, its benefits and what makes it better than other languages.

History of Python

Python has become one of the most interesting programming languages of our time. It was conceived by Guido van Rossum at CWI in the Netherlands during the late 1980's. What is peculiar about its creation is that this revolutionary program came to life out of a simple "hobby"; quoting Van Rossum. In fact, the latter intended to start this programming project with the sole purpose of entertainment and killing some time during the Christmas week of December 1989.

What is mostly amazing about this story is that he created it using solely his computer. His office was closed, and all he had was this simple machine and his brilliant mind. Thus, the first version of this program first appeared in 1991, that is 25 years ago. Python was ironically named after the famous British sketch comedy series "Monty Python's Flying Circus" as the founding father was a big fan. During the following year, the language got adopted by the team of the Amoeba project, while Guido pursued its development mainly in his spare time.

In February 1991, the first public version of Python, numbered 0.9.07, was posted on the Usenet alt. sources forum. In 1995, Van Rossum continued his work on Python at CNRI in Reston, United States, where he released several versions of the software. Whereas Python 0.6 would be the last version on Grail (an extensible Internet browser written in Python.).

Nevertheless, it does not stop here. As a matter of fact, Python continues to impress with its continuous development and progress. The development team moved to Python BeOpen.com in 2000. And that is where Python 2.0 was released.

However, it did not stop there. Python succeeded in releasing the new major version, Python 3.0, which was out in December 2008. Soon enough, this version was rapidly followed by a 3.1 version fixing the mistakes of the previous.

What is Python Mainly Used For?

Python is designed mainly to maximize the programmer's productivity by providing high-level tools and a simple syntax. It is with no doubt, a necessity for those who want to get into programming. It is considered a good language for beginners, if not the best. This is due to its great and strong static type system that a lot of programmers usually prefer over other type systems. It helps you avoid making mistakes while coding. With Its strict static types, you are indeed less likely to confuse the variables.

Python can also be used for scripting prototypes and web projects. It can as well write command line applications. It is indeed one of the few languages that embed one application in another. Actually, python gets used on different web servers handling web-hosting throughout its numerous modules. Nonetheless, it serves as a mediator between you and your computer, throughout facilitating the communication and allowing you to give orders! It could also be described as a translator, where you can interact with your computer using your pc's own language. Basically, in other words; the Python script you are going to write will not at all need any alterations or adjustments in order to be read by your computer. It rather is transferred or translated directly to your computer to be instantly understood.

To give a little glimpse at how easy this interaction is while using Python, here is a machine code used to write a sentence as simple as: (Hello world).

```
DO ,1 <- #13
PLEASE DO ,1 SUB #1 <- #238
DO ,1 SUB #2 <- #108
DO ,1 SUB #3 <- #112
DO ,1 SUB #4 <- #0
DO ,1 SUB #5 <- #64
DO ,1 SUB #6 <- #194
DO ,1 SUB #7 <- #48
PLEASE DO ,1 SUB #8 <- #22
DO ,1 SUB #9 <- #248
DO ,1 SUB #10 <- #168
DO ,1 SUB #11 <- #24
DO ,1 SUB #12 <- #16
DO ,1 SUB #13 <- #162
PLEASE READ OUT ,1
PLEASE GIVE UP
```

Whereas when it comes to writing the same sentence on python, it is much less complex, as it is showed here:

```
>>> print "Hello World"
Hello World
```

Now it's up to you to decide which script is clearer, easier and simpler!

Python is often used by system admins to create the so-called repetitive or simply maintenance tasks. Besides, if you want to create java applications by coding in Python, it now became absolutely possible. Not to mention all Python's users, such as Google (For whom Guido van Rossum has worked from 2005 to 2012), Yahoo, Microsoft, Nasa and many other popular websites such as Instagram, Pinterest, YouTube, Quora, Dropbox... etc.

What are the Benefits of Using Python?

Why would you use Python? It's because of what you actually can do with code whilst using it. Coding in simpler words is nothing but problem solving. And who wouldn't want that after all! Who wouldn't like to find solutions to everything? So at the end, it comes down to what you really want to do with it. Whatever field you're entering or working in, coding can affect and help you. And using Python specifically makes the whole process a lot easier for you.

Thanks to its excellent library, the open source code and the various online resources destined for reference and assistance, your programming will be absolutely facilitated and more transparent during the process.

One of the most important things you need to know is that over the last years, Python was entitled number one of the introductory languages. In fact, it was introduced in some of the top schools in the world, such as Stanford and MIT and many other major universities. Python became principally the language they teach. And the reason is clearly due to its simplicity. You can build in very complicated algorithms and it would remain absolutely clear and readable.

Sometimes we have to deal with a lot of information, and keeping track of them all can be quite upsetting and sometimes even impossible. Let's take the example of a shopping list for instance. You do not go out shopping holding ten pieces of papers where you've written one item on each. You make a list that includes everything. This analogy is very close to what happens when using Python; through writing in codes, we make a clear list. Hence, your life becomes more organized and a lot more coordinated. And as we all know, success only comes with good arrangements.

What makes Python better than other languages?

Python is by far the easiest language programming to learn, especially when you are a beginner and this is your first experience. It actually doesn't have main limitations; it is in fact very powerful. And the living proof to that, is the existing hundreds of success stories in major companies all around the world using python. The biggest advantage of Python is that it is easily readable. Just like reading English. Basically, reading Python is so simple and clear, that is resembles reading a book. In other words, the Python code can even be read by people who are not at all familiar with the concept of coding language.

This small example of Python coding, might illustrate the idea better:

```
>>> class Student:
...       def __init__ (self, name, age, gender):
...             self.name   = name
...             self.age    = age
...             self.gender = gender
...
>>> Sue = Student("Susan Miller", 20, "f")
>>> print Sue
<__main__.Student instance at 0x81a96cc>
>>> print Sue.age
20
```

The coding is obviously based on words from the English language, making it possible for everyone to fathom the subject matter. As we can clearly notice the words (class student, name, age, gender, self, f..). Terms that we are already familiarized with.

This advantage of a simple and accessible coding language is what keeps you motivated and encourages you to pursue your coding. Even if you get stuck on something while programming, solutions are easy to find, very simple and super easy to fathom. Moreover, once you learn the basics of coding with Python, you will be able to apply all those concepts in all the other programming languages. Whether it's C#, JavaScript (http://amzn.to/1mBhUYM), C++, Perl...Etc. Actually, no matter which programming language you're going to learn in the future, you will discover that Python's fundamentals are going to reappear over and over again and it will be an effortless learning for you.

Let's compare Python to other coding programs. Taking Java as an example. It is undeniable that the latter is easy to understand and that it has many documentations and online forums to handle all questions. Although the difference between the two resides in the fact is that Python is easier to learn from a coding perspective. Thus, Python is far less complicated than Java. You can also build new software applications more quickly.

Python applications are 20 % to 30 % of the length of a Java application, which makes the code run faster.

When it comes to TCL, however, it is known for being an application extension language, and a stand-alone programming language. Although, it has its weaknesses like every other language does. TCL is weak on data structures and similar to Java, it has slow execution of code. Not to mention the fact that it lacks features necessary for writing large programs. On the other hand, Python is known to be rapid when it comes to writing code and powerful as to wide programs and algorithms.

In this chapter you learnt about the history of Python, what it is mainly used for, its benefits and what makes it better than other languages. In the upcoming chapter you will learn how to install Python on different computer systems.

Chapter Two: Installing python

In this chapter you will learn how to install Python on Linux, Windows7/8/9/10 and on mac.

What is absolutely amazing about Python is that it could be installed on your computer no matter what type it is and operatory system it has.

Here are a few steps to follow carefully in order to help you install Python correctly. Find your computer's type, proceed, and happy installation!

Installing Python on Linux

Once your Linux machine is on, your internet connection is working, only a few steps are now separating you from installing Python. First thing to do is to open google. Write down the following "*Download Python*", or simply "*Python*".

After the results show, click on "*Download Python*" as it is demonstrated in the picture above.

You will then be directed to the python's official website "www.python.org". Since you chose the download option at first, both versions of Python are going to show for you to pick which one you wish to download.

Now scroll down the page and all the released versions of Python will show next to their release dates. In this case, you would want to click on the latest version. That is Python 3.5.0 as it shows here.

Looking for a specific release?

Python releases by version number:

Release version	Release date	
Python 3.5.0	2015-09-13	Download
Python 2.7.10	2015-05-23	Download
Python 3.4.3	2015-02-25	Download
Python 2.7.9	2014-12-10	Download
Python 3.4.2	2014-10-13	Download
Python 3.3.6	2014-10-12	Download
Python 3.2.6	2014-10-12	Download

Once opened, scroll down the page once more, and you would want to **right click** on the file *"Gzipped source tarball"*, and the chose the option *"copy link address"*.

After copying the link, all that is left for you to do now is to download it on your machine. Wait for a while, the time it gets accepted, and then you would want to type the following: "tar – xvf Python-3.5.0.tgz". You will need to test it and then configure it, this will only take a few seconds. When this operation is over, all that is left for you to do is to write down "make" which will compile the files on your machine.

This operation might take from 1 to 2 minutes, so after waiting a bit, the last step is to write down "make install" in order to finally install the file on your machine. And the installation will be successfully complete.

```
root@ubuntu:~/test/Python-3.5.0# make install
```

Python now is well installed on your machine and ready for you to use.

Installing Python on Windows 7/8/9/10

The steps I am going to show you are extremely easy, simple and manageable. All you will need now is your computer, your internet connection, and your full attention.

The first step is to go to google and write down "Python". Wait until the research is over and then click on the official python page: *Python.org*.

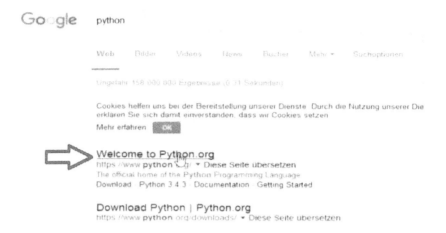

Once you have opened the page, you will need to go to the download button situated in the middle. Put your mouse on that button and then chose the "*Windows*" option.

Now you can see various options for installers. What we want in this case, is to click on the link that says "*windows x86-64executable installer*", the fifth option that is.

Python Releases for Windows

- Latest Python 2 Release - Python 2.7.10
- Latest Python 3 Release - Python 3.5.0

- Python 3.5.0 - 2015-09-13
    - Download Windows x86 web-based installer
    - Download Windows x86 executable installer
    - Download Windows x86 embeddable zip file
    - Download Windows x86-64 web-based installer
    - Download Windows x86-64 executable installer
    - Download Windows x86-64 embeddable zip file
    - Download Windows help file

Once the executable file is downloaded, you would want to open it, and the installation setup will start. Although before clicking on "*install now*", you will have to check the option that says "*Add Python 3.5 to PATH*". After checking this option, click on "*Install now*" and the installation will start.

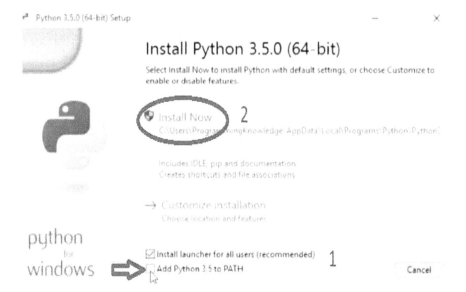

When the installation is over, close the setup window, look for the location of the file and open it. Four options are going to appear. In order to open the program, you will have to click on the second option, "*IDLE (Python 3.5 64-bit)*". And Python will be running perfectly fine.

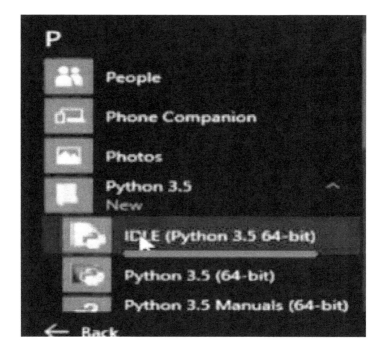

Your installation will be successful once this window is opened. And congratulations, now you officially have Python on your computer.

Installing Python on Mac

In order to install Python on your mac, you will first of all need to access to Python's official page "www.Python.org". Many buttons and options will appear. You will then need to point your mouse at the "*Downloads*" button and chose the "*Mac OS X*" Option.

Two versions of Python will appear. This is when you will decide which one to download. The latest version in this case is Python 3.5 as it shows here.

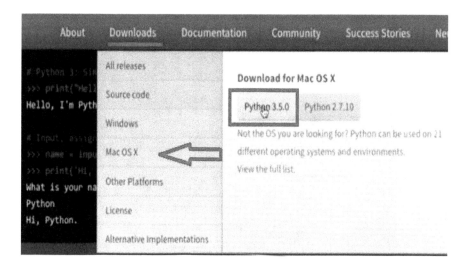

After the download process is over, open the downloaded file, and the Python's installation window will show. Click on "continue", and repeat that action, until the install button comes up. You will then click on "install".

Wait for the program to finish its installation and Python will then be accessible on your mac.

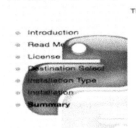

- Introduction
- Read Me
- License
- Destination Select
- Installation Type
- Installation
- Summary

The installation was successful.

The software was installed.

Close

By following these steps, you will have installed Python on your computer/mac/Linux once and for all.

Now that you have this wonderful program set up and ready to be used, it is time you followed the Instructions that will help you through it.

In this chapter you learnt about the ways to install Python on various computer systems such as (Linus, Mac, Windows7/8/9/10). In the upcoming chapter you will learn how to create your own program and how to write your first command.

Chapter Three: Introduction to programming with Python

In this chapter you will learn how to create your first program, and how to write your first command on Python.

Creating your first program

After you install Python, you need to know that it comes with a default editor and compiler. It's called "IDLE". If you are using windows, you can easily get to it, just by pressing "IDLE" in your start menu for example, or by looking for it in the program's original location. Once you find it, launch it, and this window will appear immediately.

Now this is the Python shell, those three arrows (>>>) that appear on the screen are called "Chevrons".

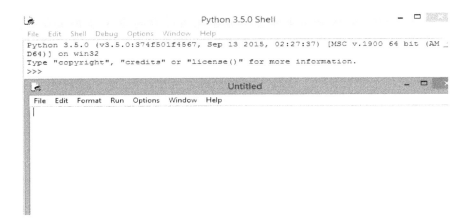

IDLE is default editor that comes with python. After you launch it, you get a start-up script, click on "File" to open a new one. This is where you are going to type your new Python program. The window is called "Untitled". It will allow you to insert your commands but it will not execute them instantly.

You need to know that Python is not a compiled or an interpreted language. That means that you can type anything into the shell and it will run immediately. It is a dynamically typed white-space-interpreted language. You can for example type down:

```
print ("hello world!")
```

And the line of code will run. Showing:

```
hello world!
>>>
```

It doesn't need any supporting files or anything of the sort. That's what makes it less complex than other languages. It just simply runs. In other words, it's a great rapid prototyping language. Therefore, if you want to start coding, then go ahead and do it, since it does not need any overhead from creating a project or anything similar. You can start immediately.

If you are on Mac, you can select IDLE from applications➔Python 3.5.

If you are on Linux, you can select IDLE from Menu ➔ Programming ➔ Python 3.5.

Writing Your First Command

Writing your first command is nothing but the beginning for you. Once you acquire this skill, you will be able to write even more complex and long programs on Python. You will learn how to run files and how to save them.

Using idle is in fact the first step towards writing your first program. If it's not running already, then launch it and then open a new file under the option File, or simply click on press Ctrl + N.

You first command will consist in writing something. First of all, you will have to write down "print" and then insert parenthesis (..). You will then need to put quotes ".." inside of those parentheses. In between, simply write your command.

For practice, enter this command in the opened "untitled" window.

```
print ("First command!")
```

26

Before running this command, you need to save your file, otherwise it will be lost. So what you are asked to do now is to go under the option "File", and select "Save file". Make sure you save it somewhere easy to find, in order to easily open it next time you will need it.

Now that your file is saved, you are in position to actually make it work! You will have to open it and then to click on "Run", select "run module" and your command will immediately be executed.

When you go back to the shell, this is the result that will show on your screen:

As a matter of fact, every time you run a module in IDLE, the shell restarts automatically.

Your first command is now affected and well executed. Why not try to modify it!

```
File    Edit    Format    Run    Options    Window    Help

print (" First command!")
print ("modifying the first command.")
```

Let's make this run once more. Although this time, you will make the process a little quicker. There is a shortcut using your keyboard that will fasten the program's execution. Press F5 and see the results for yourself.

Congratulations, you have written your first command and modified it successfully. Now that you realize how easy Python is in writing functions.

In this chapter you learnt how to write your first program and your first command. In the upcoming chapter you will learn how to use Python as a calculator.

Chapter Four: Using Python as a Calculator

In this chapter you will learn how to use Python as a calculator, manipulating numbers, variables, string values, string methods and lists.

Numbers

Python allows you to do 7 different basic arithmetic operators such as; Addition (+), subtraction (-), multiplication (*), division (/), modulus (%) and you can also make exponential calculations (**) and floor divisions (//).

First of all, we will make simple operations in the new opened file from IDLE. The process is very similar to the previous one. All you have to do is to write down: Print, and then open both the parenthesis and quotes. Insert the mathematical operation the same way you did for the text. Only this time, before closing the parenthesis, you will have to add a comma and rewrite the same operation again.

Print (number-arithmetic operator-number , number-arithmetic operator-number)

Let's take, for instance, random numbers like 5 and 4 and try to apply those mathematical operations.

```
File   Edit   Format   Run   Options

print ("5 + 4= ",5+4)
print ("5 - 4= ",5-4)
print (" 5* 4= ",5*4)
print ("5 / 4= ",5/4)
print ("5 % 4= ",5%4)
print ("5 // 4= ",5//4)
```

Now, after running the module, the calculation will be immediately executed.

You can even do more complex operations and insert them in one single coding line. Such as addition, subtraction, multiplication and division all together. Just like the following example:

```
File   Edit   Format   Run   Options   Window

print ("1+2-3*2 =" , 1+2-3*2)
|
```

We can notice that Python respected the standard order of operations for calculations, to come up with correct results:

```
                        Python 3.5.0 Shell                    – ☐  ×
File  Edit  Shell  Debug  Options  Window  Help
Python 3.5.0 (v3.5.0:374f501f4567, Sep 13 2015, 02:27:37) [MSC v.1900 64 bit (AM
D64)] on win32
Type "copyright", "credits" or "license()" for more information.
>>>
========= RESTART: C:/Users/ASUS/Desktop/Mathematical operations.py =========
1+2-3*2 = -3
>>> |
```

Whenever you are performing an arithmetic operation, you have to know that the order of operations matters. Thus, you need to know that in case you have multiplication or division, they are going to be performed before division or subtraction. This example might make it easier to understand.

```
File   Edit   Format   Run   Options   Window   F

print ("(1+2-3)*2 =" , (1+2-3)*2)|
```

This operation is very similar to the previous one we went through to test Python's calculations. Although what is different about it, is that we put braces for the addition and subtraction. Python is going to give us different values, since the multiplication is naturally going to happen first in this situation.

31

```
 ⚘                              Python 3.5.0 Shell              –  □   ✕
 File  Edit  Shell  Debug  Options  Window  Help
 Python 3.5.0 (v3.5.0:374f501f4567, Sep 13 2015, 02:27:37) [MSC v.1900 64 bit (AM
 D64)] on win32
 Type "copyright", "credits" or "license()" for more information.
 >>>
 ========= RESTART: C:/Users/ASUS/Desktop/Mathematical operations.py =========
 (1+2-3)*2 = 0
 >>> |
```

You can notice that the first value (-3) and the second (0) are distinct. This is due to the fact that Python respects the mathematical order of operations. So you better know your orders too!

Variables

Usually, when you wish to remember something in the future, be it an important phone number, a house address or an anniversary date, you write it down on a piece of paper and save it in your wallet or journals. That means that you would put the paper somewhere you would remember later on. Although, with Python, you will need variables to keep that number safe! This safe place is a variable you are going to create and associate to your number. In other words, you can consider a variable as a placeholder for something else, or some kind of a temporary storage for any value.

In order to create variables, you will need to give them a name first, and then to assign it to a value of your choosing.

So, first of all, we are going to show you how to create a very simple variable. Let's start with "X" which is a very common name for variables in Python and every other language. What we are to do now is to assign this variable to a random number, such us "8" for example. You will write X= 8 in your program and press enter. Therefore, the letter X will have the value of 8. When you are doing basic functions for instance,

32

instead of typing "8", you will simply write "X" and it will simultaneously represent that number.

File   Edit   Format   Run   Options   Window   Help

```
X=8
print (X)
```

Python

File   Edit   Shell   Debug   Options   Window   Help

```
Python 3.5.0 (v3.5.0:374f501f4567, Sep
D64)] on win32
Type "copyright", "credits" or "license
>>>
================ RESTART: C:/Users/ASUS.
8
>>> |
```

As you can clearly see, the variable is successfully recognized as 8.

In fact, you can do mathematical operations using this variable. Let's try addition, subtraction and multiplication to see what the results are going to be like.

File   Edit   Format   Run | File   Edit   Shell   Debug   Options   Window   Help

```
X= 4+4              Python 3.5.0 (v3.5.0:374f501f4567, Sep
print (X)           D64)] on win32
X= 12-4             Type "copyright", "credits" or "licens
print (X)           >>>
X= 4*2              ================ RESTART: C:/Users/ASU
print (X)           8
                    8
                    8
                    >>> |
```

33

As you can see, variables are very flexible and easy to create.

The fun part is yet to come! As a matter of fact, a variable can also contain a function!

Let's illustrate this example with a new variable, we will name it "Y". The function to this variable will be "I am Learning Python really fast". In this case you will have to write: Y = print ("I am Learning Python really fast!").

```
File   Edit   Format   Run   Options   Window   Help
Y = print ("I am Learning Python really fast !" )
print (Y)
```

And now launch it. Don't forget to use the keyboard shortcut F5!

```
File   Edit   Shell   Debug   Options   Window   Help
Python 3.5.0 (v3.5.0:374f501f4567, Sep 13 2015,
D64)] on win32
Type "copyright", "credits" or "license()" for
>>>
=========== RESTART: C:/Users/ASUS/Desktop/var:
I am Learning Python really fast !

>>> |
```

Another very fascinating thing you can do with variables is that you can unpack them.

For example, you don't feel like writing each variable and assigning it to a number or function each and every time you are working on a line. There is a better solution to write as many as you want and each will have its own value.

Let's take for example our already chosen variable X with its value of 8, and create a new one that we will call Z. We can give Z the value of the number 6.

What we are going to write now is: X , Z = (8 , 6). Python will unpack those variables and give each one its own value in the order we put them into.

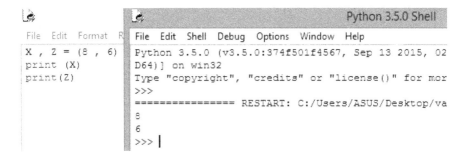

You can unpack as much variables as you want, as long as their number corresponds to the values given to them. For instance, you cannot write X , Z , G , R = (8 , 6 , 2 , 7 , 9) .

Since you have variables for numbers, mathematical operations may become so much easier than before. If you have to write a language that includes a lot of numbers and digits, you will only have to type them once in order to define the variable. Here is a little example of an addition operation where we add (8+6) without having to use the number 8, rather its variable instead.

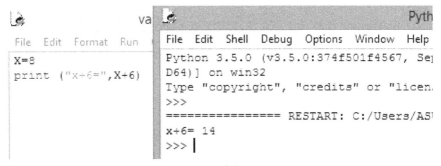

You can do the same operation using only variables. Now let's go back to our X and Z!

For a change, let's apply more than one mathematical operation this time. In this case, we will use addition, multiplication subtraction and an exponential calculation to make things more exciting.

```
File  Edit  Format  Run  C
X=8
Z=6
print ("X+Z=",X+Z)
print ("X-Z=",X-Z)
print ("X**Z=",X**Z)
```

```
File  Edit  Shell  Debug  Options  Window  Help
Python 3.5.0 (v3.5.0:374f501f4567, Sep
D64)] on win32
Type "copyright", "credits" or "license
>>>
=============== RESTART: C:/Users/ASU!
X+Z= 14
X-Z= 2
X**Z= 262144
>>>
```

You might be wondering why we would use variables when we can easily write the numbers and that this would spare us a lot of time. Well, you are right, this is an absolute waste of time in case your only numbers are 8 and 6. Although, what you must know is that variables are going to be very useful in the future when you are working on a longer program. Especially when you ignore what the value is.

All those cases we have been through are affected when you already know what the variable is going to be. Although, this is not always the case. You could be writing a program for a website, a video game or a business job and the variable's value is non-identified. In fact, it is the user of this program who is going to enter his own value. In this situation, you are going to give the variable a name and keep it in order to allow the user to fill in the missing value.

Let's say we have a variable called "W". We ignore what the value of "W" is going to be. Although, we are going to insert it in our coding. You will have to write:

W = **input** ("Enter number here please: ")

So once you pressed enter, whatever you typed in your parenthesis is going to come up and show to the user, which will allow them to insert their own value. Once the value is entered in the program, "W" will automatically be assigned to it. Let's see this little example.

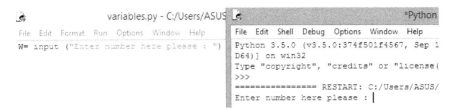

Now you have learnt how to assign a variable to a value, and how to allow others to do the same through creating the variable yourself. More is yet to come.

There is, however, a way to figure out where the value of that variable is located in python's memory. If fact, we are able to see the value's emplacement throughout the use of the id(variable) function. Once you have defined your variable and assigned it to your value, you can use the id() function in order to reach for its position in your program.

Let's keep using X as an example in order to avoid any confusions.

```
File   Edit   Shell   Debug   Options   Window   Help
Python 3.5.0 (v3.5.0:374f501f4567, Sep
D64)] on win32
Type "copyright", "credits" or "license
>>> X= 8
>>> print (X)
8
>>> id(X)
1661325264
>>> |
```

As you can see, this long number (166132....) is in fact X's location in Python's memory.

PS: The number to your variable's location is not necessarily the same as this example. It depends on your Python's memory as already mentioned.

Now this is how you can use variables. Practice assigning your variables, and using the input() function so that users can put their own values. Once you have mastered this and got used to it, you are ready to learn the next lesson.

String Values

What is a string in the first place? Do you recall our very first command? "First command!" ?

Actually that function was a string itself. A string simply is a series of characters written next to each other. You can create a string by writing a line and putting it between quotation marks. Nonetheless, one single character is considered a string as well. The same thing goes for numbers, letters, punctuation and white spaces. Probably anything you put in between quotation marks. In other words, a string that includes several characters is, as a matter of fact, a string composed of other strings!

So this is our first written string.

```
print (" First command!")
```

And this is the result it showed after launching it.

```
First command!
```

In fact, there is something you should know about strings. You can type down your command using double quotes or single quotes. Both will give the same results. For example, we can rewrite this string like the following.

```
print ('First command!')
```

And the result will remain unchanged.

```
First command!
```

Although the thing is, you cannot mix double and single quotation marks in one line. For instance, you cannot write the command as such:

```
print ("First command!')
```

Notice that the first quote is doubled, whereas the second is single. Python will immediately show this error message.

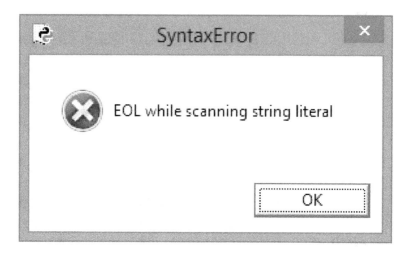

Whichever quotation marks you decide to choose; you have to commit to it in order to be able to launch your program.

You want to include quotation marks in your string? Let's say you are going to write a famous quote, and you want to include the name of the person who said it! That won't be a problem. Python is clever enough to have included this option and made it possible.

So settle on which type of quotation marks you are going to use (double/single) and then use the other one for actual quotations in your string. Look at this example:

```
File  Edit  Format  Run  Options  Window  Help
print (' "Don't cry because it's over, smile because it happened." Dr. Seuss ')
```

In this example, we used single quotes to write our string and double quotes for Dr. Seuss' words. Which gave us the following result:

40

Let's try and make something more fun with strings. We all
know what a railway looks like. Why not draw one using Python
and a simple number! First of all, we will need to make an empty
string. Our variable, in this case would be called "Railway", and
it will be declared as an empty string. Think of it as an empty
drawing paper on which you are willing to paint that railway.

As we already know, a blank space is considered a string as
well. That explains why variable's value is recognized as an
empty space after launching it.

Now let's start by adding our first trail. The variable's value
is likely to change if you define it otherwise. You can for instance
put an addition mark (+) and then insert the addition between
quotes. When you call for the variable, it will instantly show you
the new one.

41

```
File   Edit   Shell   Debug   Options   Window   Help
Python 3.5.0 (v3.5.0:374f501f4567, Sep
D64)] on win32
Type "copyright", "credits" or "license
>>> Railway = " "
>>> Railway
'  '
>>> Railway= Railway + "1"
>>> Railway
' 1'
```

Although, after modifying this variable's value, it is not possible to get the same results in case you call for it without putting the addition. This is due to the fact that Python does not store that value.

```
>>> Railway +"1"
' 11'
>>> Railway
' 1'
>>>
```

Now let's keep "Drawing" our Railway by adding a new rail each time.

File   Edit   Shell   Debug   Options   Window   Help

```
Python 3.5.0 (v3.5.0:374f501f4567, Se
D64)] on win32
Type "copyright", "credits" or "licens
>>> Railway = " "
>>> Railway
' '
>>> Railway= Railway + "1"
>>> Railway
' 1'
>>> Railway= Railway + "1"
>>> Railway
' 11'
```

This process might take a long time... Nonetheless, after doing the same thing for a while, this is the result that we finally get.

```
>>> Railway= Railway + "1"
>>> Railway
' 11111111111111111'
>>>
```

Although in order to make it shorter and straightforwardly accomplished, let's multiply that variable by 20 and see the results!

```
>>> Railway=Railway+"1"
>>> Railway
' 11'
>>> Railway= Railway + "1" *20
>>> Railway
' 11111111111111111111'
>>> |
```

You have now successfully drawn a railway using Python!

String Methods

In order to make easy modifications to strings, there are multiple methods we can use during the process. Such as: .lower(), .upper(), .replace() , .split() join(), .find("x"),and rfind("x") methods. These methods are very helpful and easy to use in order to modify your strings immediately.

- **lower():**

The first method we are going to talk about is called the upper(). Once you have entered your string, there is a possibility you render all the letters lower case characters. In this case, let's use a variable in order to make it easier to grasp. Let's call it "strMethodOne". Once you have defined your variable, you're going to use this method as it shows here:

```
File   Edit   Shell   Debug   Options   Window   Help
Python 3.5.0 (v3.5.0:374f501f4567, Sep 13 2015, 02:27:37) [MSC v
D64)] on win32
Type "copyright", "credits" or "license()" for more information.
>>> strMethodOne= "This Is The Lower Case Method"
>>> strMethodOne.lower()
'this is the lower case method'
>>> |
```

In fact, after you rewrite the variable again, you will need to put a dot "." afterwards, and this window will automatically show:

Once you have chosen the lower case and put (), the characters you inserted earlier in your variable are all going to be transformed accordingly.

As a matter of fact, this method does not affect the value of your variable in any way. For example, if you enter print(variable) in this case, you will see that it would still have the upper case. It will remain intact.

```
File  Edit  Shell  Debug  Options  Window  Help
Python 3.5.0 (v3.5.0:374f501f4567, Sep 13 2015, 02:27:37) [MSC v
D64)] on win32
Type "copyright", "credits" or "license()" for more information.
>>> strMethodOne="This Is The Lower Case Method"
>>> strMethodOne.lower()
'this is the lower case method'
>>> print (strMethodOne)
This Is The Lower Case Method
>>>
```

- **upper():**

The next method is actually very similar to this one. It is like its mirror in a way, giving it the reversed image. We call the latter: the upper case method. The techniques are practically the same. Although, instead of choosing "lower()", we will simple type down "upper()".

```
File  Edit  Shell  Debug  Options  Window  Help
Python 3.5.0 (v3.5.0:374f501f4567, Sep 13 2015, 02:27:37) [MSC v.
D64)] on win32
Type "copyright", "credits" or "license()" for more information.
>>> strMethodTwo= "this is the upper case method"
>>> strMethodTwo.upper()
'THIS IS THE UPPER CASE METHOD'
>>>
```

As you can clearly see, all the letters in our variable are transformed into capital letters.

- **replace():**

The third method we are going to talk about is the replace()
method. This one allows you to replace ay character with another.
What you would do is rewrite the variable, chose "replace", add
the parenthesis and then write down the character you would like
to replace in between quotes " " , put a comma, and write the new
character you want to put instead. It goes like this :
       variable . replace("character to replace" , "new character")

       Let's go for our variable, replace the letter "t" with the
letter "k" and see what would happen!

```
File  Edit  Shell  Debug  Options  Window  Help
Python 3.5.0 (v3.5.0:374f501f4567, Sep 13 2015, 02:27:37) [MSC v.:
D64)] on win32
Type "copyright", "credits" or "license()" for more information.
>>> strMethodThree="this is the replace method"
>>> strMethodThree.replace("t", "k")
'khis is khe replace mekhod'
>>> |
```

       As you can clearly see, the letter "t" was successfully
replaced by the letter "k".

- **split():**

       The next method is called split. It is very simple, and
extremely useful. It splits every white space it finds, making by
which the characters clearer and more distinguished to the eye.
The operation is quite the same; you write your variable and you
put split after the dot; .split .

47

```
File  Edit  Shell  Debug  Options  Window  Help
Python 3.5.0 (v3.5.0:374f501f4567, Sep 13 2015,
D64)] on win32
Type "copyright", "credits" or "license()" for
>>> strMethodFour="This is the split method"
>>> strMethodFour.split()
['This', 'is', 'the', 'split', 'method']
>>> |
```

There are many other options included in this method. In fact, you can choose which exact sequence to split. For example, let's say we want to split this string in the first two and leave it the way it is for the second part. You open up your parenthesis, put a blank space between the quotes, and the number of the parts to split.

```
>>> strMethodFour.split(" " , 2)
['This', 'is', 'the split method']
>>> |
```

• join():

For our fifth method: .join (), is a little bit different from the previous methods. This one consists mainly in joining lists (which we will clarify afterwards) or any sequences that you want by using a string you would provide. Like for example "/" or " ", "*"..etc.

So this method, unlike the ones that preceded, would actually start by the sequence you would want to add between quotes. "sequence to join" join (the list you created)

```
File  Edit  Shell  Debug  Options  Window  Help
Python 3.5.0 (v3.5.0:374f501f4567, Sep 13 2015,
D64)] on win32
Type "copyright", "credits" or "license()" for ɪ
>>> strMethodFive="This is the join method"
>>> "*".join(strMethodFive)
'T*h*i*s* *i*s* *t*h*e* *j*o*i*n* *m*e*t*h*o*d'
>>> |
```

- **find("x"):**

Our sixth method is called: .find ("x") method. This one helps you find the index location of the first occurrence of a character of your choice in your string. Our string would be "This is the find method. And we are going to look for the location of the first occurrence of the letter "i".

```
File  Edit  Shell  Debug  Options  Window  Help
Python 3.5.0 (v3.5.0:374f501f4567, Sep 13 2015, 02:27:37) [MSC v
D64)] on win32
Type "copyright", "credits" or "license()" for more information.
>>> strMethodSix="This is the find method"
>>> strMethodSix.find ("i")
2
```

The result for the index location of the letter "i" is shown through the result 2 for its occurrence.

- **rfind("x"):**

Another similar method to this one is called: .rfind("x"). This method, however, returns the last index location of the character you have chosen. Just like the following.

49

```
File   Edit   Shell   Debug   Options   Window   Help
Python 3.5.0 (v3.5.0:374f501f4567, Sep 13 2
D64)] on win32
Type "copyright", "credits" or "license()"
>>> strMethodSix="This is the find method"
>>> strMethodSix.find ("i")
2
>>> strMethodSix.rfind("i")
13
>>> |
```

As you can see, 13 is the number of the occurrence of the last location of the character "i".

So these are the most needed methods while working with strings. They are extremely helpful and absolutely important for anyone who would work on any kind of program.

Lists

A list is one of the most powerful data structures in Python. It is a sequence that includes many things. It could be a list of integers, of characters, letters, words, or shortly, anything you would want to put in it. All you have to do in order to create a list is to put the elements into brackets "[ ]". Press on "alt gr + (" at the same time for the first bracket " [" and "alt gr+ ")" for the second to close it .

So let's create a new variable, and call it "ListOne". ListOne is going to include integers such as: 1,2,3,4 and 5. Our list would look like this:

```
File   Edit   Shell   Debug   Options   Window   Help
Python 3.5.0 (v3.5.0:374f501f4567, Sep
D64)] on win32
Type "copyright", "credits" or "licens
>>> ListOne=[1,2,3,4,5,]
>>> |
```

Now, if you want to call for the first element in the list, you would need to type the following:

```
File   Edit   Shell   Debug   Options   Window   Help
Python 3.5.0 (v3.5.0:374f501f4567, Sep
D64)] on win32
Type "copyright", "credits" or "licens
>>> ListOne=[1,2,3,4,5]
>>> ListOne [0]
1
>>> |
```

ListOne [0]. As a matter of fact, in Python, or in any other language, the first element of a list is considered to be the 0th element instead of the 1st. Therefore, the first element in our list would be the integer "2", the second would be "3" etc.

```
File   Edit   Shell   Debug   Options   Window   Help
Python 3.5.0 (v3.5.0:374f501f4567, Sep
D64)] on win32
Type "copyright", "credits" or "license
>>> ListOne=[1,2,3,4,5]
>>> ListOne[1]
2
>>> |
```

So this is how you would refer to elements in a Python's list.

Now, the thing about lists is that they could include any element you wish to put in them. More to that, you could mix characters, strings and integers and put them the same list.

For instance, you could take the variable we created, and redefine some of the elements in it. In our case, let's take the 3rd element which would be "4" and reset it to be a text of our choice.

```
File   Edit   Shell   Debug   Options   Window   Help
Python 3.5.0 (v3.5.0:374f501f4567, Sep
D64)] on win32
Type "copyright", "credits" or "licens
>>> ListOne=[1,2,3,4,5]
>>> ListOne[3]
4
>>> |
```

So this is our 3rd element. In order to insert whichever character, string or integer, you would have to do the same thing with variables. After all it's a slight modification of an element. Now let's redefine it with the following text "I can manipulate lists easily".

```
Python 3.5.0 (v3.5.0:374f501f4567, Sep 13 2015,
D64)] on win32
Type "copyright", "credits" or "license()" for r
>>> ListOne=[1,2,3,4,5]
>>> ListOne[3]
4
>>> ListOne[3]= "I can manipulate lists easily"
>>> print (ListOne)
[1, 2, 3, 'I can manipulate lists easily', 5]
>>> |
```

What is even more interesting about lists, is that you can create a list Within another!
Remember the famous E.A Poe's poem "A dream within a dream"? well, Python is THAT poetic as well, or so it seems! Indeed, you can for example redefine the 0th element, that is the integer "1" and redefine it as a new list of your own choosing. Let's reset this element with a list that would include [-1,-2,-3,-4,-5].

The result would be :

```
[1, 2, 3, 'I can manipulate lists easily', 5]
>>> ListOne[0]=[-1,-2,-3,-4,-5]
>>> ListOne
[[-1, -2, -3, -4, -5], 2, 3, 'I can manipulate lists easily', 5]
>>> |
```

As you can see, the 0th element now refers to the new data structure, and the variable is successfully redefined.

Now let's say that you want to create a new variable and give it the same value as the first one. Which means that both lists are going to include the same elements. Our new variable would be called "ListTwo". We would want ListTwo to have the same value as ListOne.

```
>>> ListTwo=ListOne
>>> ListTwo
[[-1, -2, -3, -4, -5], 2, 3, 'I can manipulate lists easily', 5]
>>> |
```

ListTwo now shares the same value as our first variable. That leads us to the fact that in case we change the value of either of the variables, we are changing them both at the same time. For instance, if we change the 4th element in ListTwo, the new redefined value would be simultaneously changed for ListOne.

```
>>> ListTwo[4]=["I am changing this element"]
>>> print (ListTwo)
[[-1, -2, -3, -4, -5], 2, 3, 'I can manipulate lists easily', ['I am changing this element']
]
>>> print (ListOne)
[[-1, -2, -3, -4, -5], 2, 3, 'I can manipulate lists easily', ['I am changing this element']
]
>>> |
```

This operation, though, is not copying, rather creating two variables and giving them the exact same values.

However, for copying you would need to take a different path. In this case, let's create a third variable called "ListThree". You would need to write down: ListThree= ListOne[:] Which means that your new variable would be the copy of the already defined one from the beginning to the end.

```
>>> ListThree=ListOne[:]
>>> ListThree
[[-1, -2, -3, -4, -5], 2, 3, 'I can manipulate lists easily', ['I am changing this element']
]
>>> |
```

You could also copy a list all with imposing your own conditions. For example, let's create another list we call "ListFour" and only copy elements up to the 3rd. Meaning, this list will include the values of the first as long as it is up to this element but not including it.

PS: To refresh your memory, ListOne goes like this:

[[-1, -2, -3, -4, -5], 2, 3, 'I can manipulate lists easily', ['I am changing this element']]

So our new variable; ListFour would include those values.

```
>>> ListFour=ListOne[0:3]
>>> ListFour
[[-1, -2, -3, -4, -5], 2, 3]
>>> |
```

You can notice that the values it held are the 0th, 1st and 2nd only. Thus, our condition was well executed.

It's amazing how you can create variables, define lists and manipulate them using very simple and easy techniques. Along with copying them and imposing your own conditions. These techniques are in fact absolutely useful and can come in handy while writing your programs.

Congratulations, you have succeeded creating lists and managed many Python techniques.
Embrace yourself for the next chapter!

In this chapter you learnt about how to use Python as a calculator, including numbers, variables, string values, string methods and lists. In the upcoming chapter you will learn about the control flow tools such as the if statement, elif statement and the if else statement.

Chapter Five: Control Flow Tools

In this chapter you will learn how to use the if statement, the else statement and the elif statement.

If Statement

Adding logic to your program is very useful in writing more complex and practical language. In this case, we are going to show you how to type down a very basic form of logic called the if statements. The if statement is used in order to check to see if something is the case. If it is so, it will execute your command, otherwise, it will simply continue along and execute you other requests. We are going to apply this method while using one of the most common operators in our example; ">", "<", "=".

Let's choose the variable X and assign the number 8 to it: X=6, and another variable Y=3. After presenting our variables, we are going to write down the if statement and see if the operation is executable.

```
File   Edit   Format   Run   Options   Window   |

X=6
Y=3
if X>Y:
      print ("X is greater than Y")
```

As we can see, X is actually greater than Y, therefore, our command is going to be executed correctly in this case.

```
Python 3.5.0 (v3.5.0:374f501f4567, Sep
D64)] on win32
Type "copyright", "credits" or "licens
>>>
=============== RESTART: C:/Users/ASUS
X is greater than Y
>>> |
```

Although, if we try and inverse this operation, where we ask to see if X is less than Y, there won't be any execution in this case.

The command was obviously not executed, since in our example, the variable X is greater than Y. (6<3).

What we are going to do now is to add another variable. Let's call it Z. The variable Z is going to have the same value as Y assigned to it. Thus, Z=3. Now let's compare Z, X and Z altogether and see if our command is going to be executed.

File   Edit   Format   Run   Options   Window   Help

```
X=6
Y=3
Z=3
if Z<X>Y:
    print ("X is greater than Z and greater than Y")
```

This operation is correct, which is why the command is going to be executed immediately.

File	Edit	Shell	Debug	Options	Window	Help

```
Python 3.5.0 (v3.5.0:374f501f4567, Sep 1:
D64)] on win32
Type "copyright", "credits" or "license(;
>>>
=================== RESTART: C:/Users/AS(
X is greater than Z and greater than Y
>>> |
```

There is another thing you can also do with those operators. Let's check if is less than or equal to X.

File	Edit	Format	Run	Options	Window	Help

```
X=6
Y=3
Z=3
if Z<=X:
    print ("Z is less than or equal to X")
```

Knowing that it's the case, after launching it, the result is going to be:

```
File   Edit   Shell   Debug   Options   Window   Help
Python 3.5.0 (v3.5.0:374f501f4567, Sep
D64)] on win32
Type "copyright", "credits" or "licens
>>>
================== RESTART: C:/Users/
Z is less than or equal to X
>>> |
```

Although if you want to see if two values are equal to each other, you cannot use the equal sign the same way you are using greater than and less than operators "<" or ">" in the if statement.

Because in this case, you will look like you are comparing two variables to each other Z=Y. Thus, you are going to need to put a double equal sign as it follows: Z==Y

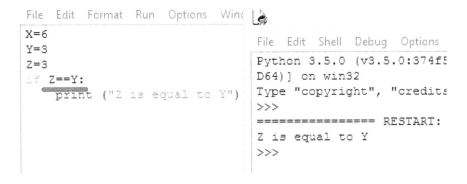

Another way to do it, if you want to check if it does not hold the same value, a not equal sign that is, you will have to put both an exclamation mark and an equal sign: !=

59

```
X=6
Y=3
Z=3
if Z!=X:
    print ("Z is equal to X")
```

```
File   Edit   Shell   Debug   Options   Window   Help
Python 3.5.0 (v3.5.0:374f501f4567, Sep
D64)] on win32
Type "copyright", "credits" or "license
>>>
=============== RESTART: C:\Users\ASUS\
Z is equal to X
>>> |
```

So those are the basics to the if statement, it is indeed a very simple statement, and you can also add many things to it, which we will see in the if else statement.

If Else Statement

The idea of the if else statement, is to add one more step of logic to your usage of the if statement. So with this statement, we get to decide what to do next if the command we typed is not the case. In other words, the program will be launched automatically in both cases, whether our statement is correct or not.

So let's use the same variables we defined earlier and see how this else statement functions!

Let's say that we will check whether or not X<Y (X=6/Y=3)

If it is the case, the program will show "X is less than Y", otherwise, it will show "X is not less than Y".

```
X=6
Y=3
Z=3
if X<Y:
    print ("X is less than Y")
else:
    print ("X is not less than Y")
```

```
Python 3.5.0 (v3.5.0:374f501f4567, Sep 1
D64)] on win32
Type "copyright", "credits" or "license(
>>>
================ RESTART: C:\Users\ASUS\
X is not less than Y
>>>
```

Since we already know that the first condition is not logical, Python directly executed the second condition. Therefore, it showed our sccond command that is "X is not less than Y".

In fact, we can put more than one condition at the same time, and Python will still run correctly, executing all of our conditions.

For instance, we can add another condition to see if x is less than 90.

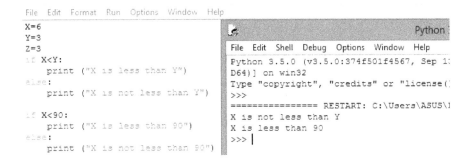

```
X=6
Y=3
Z=3
if X<Y:
    print ("X is less than Y")
else:
    print ("X is not less than Y")

if X<90:
    print ("X is less than 90")
else:
    print ("X is not less than 90")
```

```
Python 3.5.0 (v3.5.0:374f501f4567, Sep 1:
D64)] on win32
Type "copyright", "credits" or "license(
>>>
================ RESTART: C:\Users\ASUS\
X is not less than Y
X is less than 90
>>>
```

Python execute both commands while using the else statement at first and the if condition next, according to the conditions we imposed.

Elif Statement

The idea of the Elif statement is to add yet another step of logic to our pre-existing if and else statements. Normally, while using the latter two statements, you check one line and have it run otherwise if it fails to run using the else statement. But what if you want to use multiple if statements? Wouldn't be a waste of time to check each one on its own and rewrite the whole process over again? This is where the Elif statement intervenes. It allows you to run multiple conditions while avoiding the usage of the else statement at each step. Let's go back to our variables: X=6 / Y=3 / Z=3

We will check if X is less than Z. Knowing that it's going to fail, we will put an else statement. Although before proceeding, we will add another condition, the Elif condition that is, in order to check if X is greater than Y. We are certain, however, that the second condition is definitely going to run.

```
File  Edit  Format  Run  Options  Window  Help
X=6
Y=3
Z=3
if X<Z:
    print ("X is less than Z")

elif X>Y:

    print ("X is greater than Y")
else:
|
    print ("The else condition is not going to be triggered")
```

We already know that the first will not run since 6>3, thus X is greater than Z, not less than it. Whereas for the other results:

```
Python 3.5.0 (v3.5.0:374f501f4567, Se]
D64)] on win32
Type "copyright", "credits" or "licen.
>>>
================== RESTART: C:/Users.
X is greater than Y
>>> |
```

The first statement did not run, since it's illogical, the second, however, was launched since X is indeed greater than Y. Which didn't trigger the Else statement. In case the first condition (if statement) and the second (elif statement) both didn't run, then the else statement would be launched automatically.

As a matter of fact, you also have the possibility to include more than one elif statement, for example, let's keep our already written program, and add another condition before the else statement:

```
X=6
Y=3
Z=3
if X<Z:
    print ("X is less than Z")
elif X>Y:

    print ("X is greater than Y")
elif 50<100:

    print ("50 is less than 100")
else:

    print ("The else condition is not going to be triggered")
```

You might think that both elif statements are going to run, although that will not be the case:

```
File   Edit   Shell   Debug   Options   Window   Help
Python 3.5.0 (v3.5.0:374f501f4567, Sep
D64)] on win32
Type "copyright", "credits" or "licens
>>>
================== RESTART: C:/Users/
X is greater than Y
>>> |
```

As you can clearly see, the program came up with the same result as earlier. Even though we all know that 50 is in fact less than 100. The reason it did not run, is because once the first elif statement was triggered as true, Python simply stopped searching for something to run. It's like it is looking for one true answer, once it gets it, it just stops asking.

In this chapter you learnt how to use the if statement, else statement and elif statement. In the upcoming chapter you will learn about loops.

Chapter Six: Chapter Six: Loops

In this chapter you will learn about Loops, which includes both options; the for loop, the while loop and the True loop.

Generally, Python executes statements in a specific order. For instance, in a function, the first statement is executed first, followed by the second and third and so it goes subsequently. Although, sometimes, you realize that you need to run those statements many times. Which is mainly what both for and while loops are used for.

For Loops

In order to better clarify the for loop's role in writing your program, we are going to illustrate it using a list. Like the one we have been over in the fourth chapter. After you create your list, you will have to write: for the_name_of_the_variable in name_of_the_list :

```
File  Edit  Format  Run  Optio

OurList=[1,5,9,8,6,3,7]
for X in OurList:
    print (X)
```

```
Python

File  Edit  Shell  Debug  Options  Window  Help

Python 3.5.0 (v3.5.0:374f501f4567, Sep 1
D64)] on win32
Type "copyright", "credits" or "license(
>>>
================ RESTART: C:\Users\ASUS\
1
5
9
8
6
3
7
>>> |
```

As you can see, it iterated throughout the entire list in the good order.

You need to know that respecting the indentation is of an extreme importance when it comes to loops.

For example, if we add a string to this loop without the indentation, it will show as such:

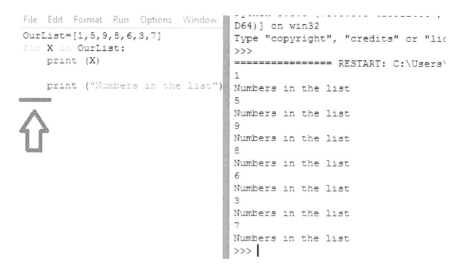

Whereas, if you respect the indentation, the result will be completely different from the previous one.

In this case, as we can clearly see, that the string "Numbers in the list" is repeated before every number.

Now let's try to apply the for loop on a different sequence. A month per say. We will choose "month" as our defined string, and we will name our variable "Letter".

```
File  Edit  Format  Run  Opti    >>>
Month= "Novepmber"              =============== RESTART: C:\Users\ASUS\Desk
for Letter in Month:            N
    print (Letter)              o
                                v
                                e
                                p
                                m
                                b
                                e
                                r
                                >>> |
```

In fact, there is another function in python that could help us make could use of the for loop. This function is called the range() function. This function takes two values: range (start value,end value): This function, combined with the for loop allows you to print the numbers from the start value to the end value. Like this example:

```
File  Edit  Format  Run  Opti    >>>
for X in range (1,11):          =============== RESTART: C:
    print (X)                   1
                                2
                                3
                                4
                                5
                                6
                                7
                                8
                                9
                                10
                                >>> |
```

As we can see, the for loop and range function generated the list of numbers from 1 to 10 after the execution of the program. You can notice that the number 11 in non-existent in the list. This is due to the fact that in that case, it only goes from the first number up to the last.

While Loops

A while loop is used to perform an operation while you set your own conditions. Let's set our condition by defining a variable first. Our value will be called "condition", and the value assigned to it is 2. Condition = 2. We are going to use the while loop setting the condition that it adds 1 during every step of the way until it is less than 10.

```
File  Edit  Format  Run  Options  Window
condition = 2
while condition <10:
    print (condition)

    condition = condition + 1
```

```
Type "copyright", "credits
>>>
================ RESTART:
2
3
4
5
6
7
8
9
>>> |
```

It obviously stopped at the number 9 since 10 is clearly equals to 10 and not less. Therefore, the condition is fulfilled using that loop.

While True

By setting a condition to the while loop, it executed the task according to that condition. That means that it is an infinite loop which will break once the condition is fulfilled. Although if you

68

want to loop to be infinite, there is another option to it that is called: while True ( ):

This will start running the sequence you entered infinitely, it will not stop until you break the loop yourself. So in this case, we are going to use the while true loop with the if statement in order to limit it. Our variable will be X. and its assigned value will be 8. X=8. Another thing we can use is the function "Break". Which will automatically break it out of the program. And the function "continue" to proceed the action we asked for.

```
File  Edit  Format  Run  Op        File  Edit  Shell  Debug  Options  Window  Help
X=8                                 Python 3.5.0 (v3.5.0:374f501f4567, Sep
while True:                         D64)] on win32
    X=X+2                           Type "copyright", "credits" or "license
    if X>15:                        >>>
        break                       =============== RESTART: C:\Users\ASUS
    else:                           10
        print (X)                   12
        continue                    14
                                    >>> |
```

Clearly, the loop was broken when X became equal to 15, since our condition stated that it must be greater than that number.

In this chapter you learnt how to use the while loop and the for loop including the if statements and conditions.

In the upcoming chapter you will learn about the defining functions.

Chapter Seven: Defining functions

In this chapter you will learn about functions, their parameters, their parameter defaults, the pass statement, the default parameters for arguments and the keyword arguments.

Function Parameters

The idea of a function is to assign a set of code and possibly variables that are known as parameters to a single text. Thus, instead of writing your program every time you want to execute it, you will just write the name of your function and it will automatically be running. In order to begin writing a function, you need to define it using the keyword: def (which is a short for define). Do it goes like this: def function's name () :

In our case, let's choose the name (FirstFunction)!

File   Edit   Format   Run   Options   Window   Help

```
def FirstFunction ():
    print ("This is our first example of a function")
    print ("Functions are easy to learn")
    print ("Python is not hard after all")
    X= ("This is a simple" + " " +"programming language")
    print (X)
```

So now we have defined our function and filled it with strings and a variable containing other strings. Although when we run the program, notice that the function is not going to be executed.

```
File   Edit   Shell   Debug   Options   Window   Help

Python 3.5.0 (v3.5.0:374f501f4567, Se
D64)] on win32
Type "copyright", "credits" or "licen:
>>>
=================== RESTART: C:/Users,
>>> |
```

You must be thinking that we did something wrong while writing the function. Although, the thing is, we defined the function, but we did not call for it in the program. So every time you want to call for your function, you will have to type it down into the shell and it will automatically be executed.

```
File   Edit   Shell   Debug   Options   Window   Help

Python 3.5.0 (v3.5.0:374f501f4567, Sep 1
D64)] on win32
Type "copyright", "credits" or "license(
>>>
=================== RESTART: C:\Users\AS
>>> FirstFunction ()
This is our first example of a function
Functions are easy to learn
Python is not hard after all
This is a simple programming language
>>> |
```

Another thing you can do, is to type it down on your file after defining it, although it does not follow the same order of lining of its own definition process. As it follows:

```
def FirstFunction ():
    print ("This is our first example of a function")
    print ("Functions are easy to learn")
    print ("Python is not hard after all")
    X= ("This is a simple" + " " +"programming language")
    print (X)

FirstFunction ()
```

Python 3.5.0 Shell

```
Python 3.5.0 (v3.5.0:374f501f4567, Sep 13 2015, 02:27:37)
D64)] on win32
Type "copyright", "credits" or "license()" for more inform
>>>
=================== RESTART: C:\Users\ASUS\Desktop\both.py
This is our first example of a function
Functions are easy to learn
Python is not hard after all
This is a simple programming language
>>> |
```

You can actually add more options to your function. What we are going to show you now mainly consists in defining your function and adding variables within the braces. Let's for example do some addition and subtraction operations. Name our variables X and Y, and then proceed with the execution!

```
def SecondFunction (X,Y)
    Operation1 = X +Y
    print ("X is", X)
    print ("Y is ", Y)
    print (Operation1)
    Operation2= X-Y
    print(Operation2)
SecondFunction (6,3)
```

```
Python 3.5.0 (v3.5.0:374f501f4567, Sep
D64)] on win32
Type "copyright", "credits" or "licens
>>>
================ RESTART: C:\Users\ASU
X is 6
Y is  3
9
3
>>> |
```

72

As you can see, the variables took place within the order we assigned to them. In case you were confused and needed to make sure the variables are correct, you can define them once more as it follows:

```
File  Edit  Format  Run  Options  Window  Help
def SecondFunction (X,Y):
    Operation1 = X + Y
    print ("X is", X)
    print ("Y is", Y)
    print (Operation1)
    Operation2 = X-Y
    print (Operation2)


SecondFunction (X=6,Y=3)
```

```
Pytho
File  Edit  Shell  Debug  Options  Window  Help
Python 3.5.0 (v3.5.0:374f501f4567, Sep
D64)] on win32
Type "copyright", "credits" or "license
>>>
================== RESTART: C:/Users/I
X is 6
Y is 3
9
3
>>> |
```

This could be very useful if you are defining a function that includes many variables and they are more complicated than just a simple 9 and a 3.

Pass Statement

Let's suppose that you have a function to define, but you remembered something more important and urgent to write down first, Python has an option called pass. You can define your function and name it, and then type pass, write the other programming task and then you can go back to it by rewriting it again.

You can use this option if you're going to write another variable, string, list, characters or basically anything you like, and even defining a new function is going to work out for you.

```
File  Edit  Format  Run  Options  Window  Help
def SecondFunction (X,Y):
    pass
def ThirdFunction (Z,W):
    print ("This function will be executed")
    print ("Z is equal to ", Z)
    print ("W is equal to", W)
ThirdFunction(4,5)
```

```
File  Edit  Shell  Debug  Options  Window  Help
Python 3.5.0 (v3.5.0:374f501f4567, Sep
D64)] on win32
Type "copyright", "credits" or "license
>>>
================ RESTART: C:\Users\ASUS
This function will be executed
Z is equal to   4
W is equal to 5
>>> |
```

As you can see, our second function has been executed conveniently, and our first was considered as a null operation. This could help you when you don't want to forget defining a function even if you still ignore the variables and their values in order to fill it.

```
def SecondFunction (X,Y):
    pass
print ("I have something else to write")
```

```
Python 3.5.0 (v3.5.0:374f501f4567, Sep 1
D64)] on win32
Type "copyright", "credits" or "license(
>>>
=================== RESTART: C:/Users/AS
I have something else to write
>>> |
```

Default parameters

While defining our function, we can actually assign a value to our arguments at the beginning of the process. For example, we can write a function about someone's weight and age, and already give out one of those value in advance. As it follows:

```
File  Edit  Format  Run  Options  Wi
def DefaultFunction (W,A=35)
    print(W,A)
    print("Weight is ", W)
    print("Age is", A)
DefaultFunction (150)
```

```
File  Edit  Shell  Debug  Options  Window  Help
Python 3.5.0 (v3.5.0:374f501f4567, Sep 1
D64)] on win32
Type "copyright", "credits" or "license
>>>
================ RESTART: C:\Users\ASUS\
150 35
Weight is  150
Age is 35
>>> |
```

As you can see, the program ran automatically after defining the first variable at first, and the second at last. This is due to the fact that it had a default value to it. You could use this default parameter when you ignore what the argument is going to be.

Default Values For Arguments

Let's say for example, you are working on a program for a web site, and you want to ask what the gender of the person is, male or female. What you're going to do is to use a function along with the if, and elif statements.

```
File   Edit   Format   Run   Options   Window   He

def What_gender (Gender="Unknown"):
    if Gender is "m":
        Gender = "male"
    elif Gender is "f":
        Gender="female"

    print (Gender)

What_gender("m")
What_gender ("f")
What_gender ()
```

Since we ignore what the gender of that person is going to be, we set a default value for that matter. We also added "Unknown" in order to fill in the empty space in case there was no answer provided.

While calling for the program, we set our options, if it's a male, they will enter "m", if it's a female it will be "f", and if they don't type anything, the gender is going to be Unknown.

This is the result we get after launching this program.

```
File   Edit   Shell   Debug   Options

Python 3.5.0 (v3.5.0:374f!
D64)] on win32
Type "copyright", "credit:
>>>
================== RESTAI
male
female
Unknown
>>> |
```

Keyword Arguments

First of all, let's start writing our function using the default values for arguments that we saw previously in order to be able to apply our modifications later on, using the keyword arguments method. Our function will different from the one preceding it. We will simply write a sentence and play on words.

```
File   Edit   Format   Run   Options   Window   Help

def Sentence(Subject="I",Verb="love",Noun="Python"):
    print(Subject,Verb,Noun)
Sentence()
```

In this function, we only used default arguments, and the result after launching it is of course the following:

```
File   Edit   Shell   Debug   Options   Window   Help
Python 3.5.0 (v3.5.0:374f501f4567, Sep
D64)] on win32
Type "copyright", "credits" or "licens
>>>
=================== RESTART: C:\Users\.
I love Python
>>> |
```

However, what we are going to do to this function is more than that. Now whenever we want to pass new parameters, Python is going to set them in the order we first put (Subject, Verb, Noun).

For example, if we write a different sentence, like this one:

```
File   Edit   Format   Run   Options   Window   Help
def Sentence(Subject="I",Verb="love",Noun="Python"):
    print(Subject,Verb,Noun)
Sentence()
Sentence("Python","is","awesome")
|
```

The function we created earlier named "Sentence" takes three variables. And since we are passing through another three strings variables right now in our sentence (Python is awesome), Python is going to assign each Item following the orders we set. Thus the result is going to be:

```
File   Edit   Shell   Debug   Options   Window   Help

Python 3.5.0 (v3.5.0:374f501f4567, Sep 13
D64)] on win32
Type "copyright", "credits" or "license()
>>>
=================== RESTART: C:\Users\ASU.
I love Python
Python is awesome
>>> |
```

Although if you want to pass it in a different order, what you will have to do is to use the keyword of the argument you put at the beginning while defining your function. Let's say we would like to change the orderly positions of our parameters.

```
File   Edit   Format   Run   Options   Window   Help

def Sentence(Subject="I",Verb="love",Noun="Python"):
    print(Subject,Verb,Noun)
Sentence()
Sentence("Python","is","awesome")
Sentence (Noun="great",Verb="is", Subject="This")
|
```

After changing the order of the items, the result is the following:

```
File   Edit   Shell   Debug   Options   Window   Help

Python 3.5.0 (v3.5.0:374f501f4567, Sep
D64)] on win32
Type "copyright", "credits" or "license
>>>
=================== RESTART: C:\Users\A
I love Python
Python is awesome
This is great
>>> |
```

In this last chapter you learnt how to define functions, use function parameters, pass statements, default value for arguments and keyword arguments.

Congratulations! You have now completed this step-by-step guide and have gained tremendous knowledge on Python!

Turn to next page to see a quick recap of what we have covered in this book.

Here is a quick recap of what we covered in case you need a refresher on a certain step:

1. You now have an understanding of Python and how to use it conveniently.
2. You learnt how to install it with different computer systems.
3. You learnt how to create your first program and write your first command.
4. You learnt how to use to use Python as a calculator (numbers, variables, string values, lists).
5. You learnt how to use control flow tools (if statements, if else statement, elif statement).
6. You learnt how to manipulate loops (for loop, while loop, while True loop).
7. You learnt how to define functions.
8. You also learnt how to use pass statements, default parameters, default parameters for arguments and keyword arguments.

Turn to the next page to gain access to a free video course and to also see my other best-selling books part of this series!

Before You Go

First of all, I want to congratulate you for the efforts you made while reading this book, and your will and determination in learning this absolutely amazing programming language.

As you can see, Python is absolutely simple and extremely easy for a coding language. You can effortlessly write any kind of program, and it is a guaranteed success. Not only is it fathomable and clear, but it also has many advantages on so many levels.

Challenge yourself and spend more time practicing and repeating the examples we showed you. For we all know that practice makes perfect, and perfection is at your fingertips.

After acquiring this knowledge, you should consider yourself already a programmer. I urge you to learn other programming languages so that you may be able to take your knowledge to the next and become a top-class programmer and because you have gone through this course, you will be astonished to find that your learning other languages is easier than expected, for Python has strikingly paved the way for you. You can find other popular programming books by visiting our full library at >> http://amzn.to/1Xxmab2

I would also really appreciate your reviews and your feedback. If you really enjoyed this book, then feel free to share it so other people may also profit from this information.

Please visit http://amzn.to/1TIRHGk to leave a review!

Before You Go, Here Are Other Books Our Readers Loved!

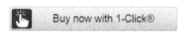

Learn JavaScript Programming Today With This Easy Step-By-Step Guide!

Buy now with 1-Click®

http://amzn.to/1mBhUYM

Learn C Programming Today With This Easy, Step-By-Step Guide

NEW

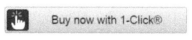
Buy now with 1-Click®

http://amzn.to/1Wl6fHu

Learn R Programming
With This Easy,
Step-By-Step Guide

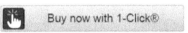

http://amzn.to/24XxoLM

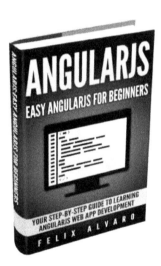

Learn AngularJS
Web-App Developing
Today With This Easy,
Step-By-Step Guide

http://amzn.to/1pDq0BZ

Learn Java Programming
Today With This Easy,
Step-By-Step Guide!

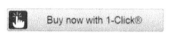

http://amzn.to/1WTgUw0

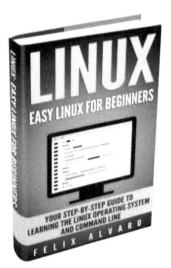

Learn The Linux Operating
System and Command
Line Today!

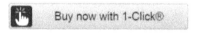

http://amzn.to/1QzQPkY

All You Need To Learn
To Drive Tons Of Traffic
To Your Website Today!

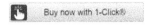

http://amzn.to/21HWFWb

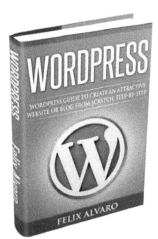

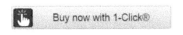

Easily Create Your Own
Eye-Catching, Professional
Website or Blog Using
WordPress Today!

http://amzn.to/1VHtxZi

Launch Your Own Profitable eBay Business- Learn Everything You Need to Know to Get Started Today!

http://amzn.to/1R1vnCP

Finally, you can also send me an email if you have any questions, feedback or just want to say hello! (I do reply!) My email address is; (Felix_Alvaro@mail.com)

I thank you once again and God bless!

Felix Alvaro

www.ingramcontent.com/pod-product-compliance
Lightning Source LLC
LaVergne TN
LVHW052309060326
832902LV00021B/3789